On the Edge

ROBIN FORD

Cinnamon Press
Independent Innovative International

Published by Cinnamon Press
Meirion House
Glan yr afon
Tanygrisiau
Blaenau Ffestiniog
Gwynedd
LL41 3SU
www.cinnamonpress.com

The right of Robin Ford to be identified as author of this work has been asserted by him in accordance with the Copyright, Designs and Patent Act, 1988. Copyright © 2010 Robin Ford
978-1-907090-01-1
British Library Cataloguing in Publication Data. A CIP record for this book can be obtained from the British Library.

Designed and typeset in Palatino by Cinnamon Press. Cover design by Mike Fortune-Wood from original artwork by 'Isle of Wight Seascape' by biginfocus
Printed by MPG Books Group, Kings Lynn & Bodmin.

Cinnamon Press is represented in the UK by Inpress Ltd www.inpressbooks.co.uk and in Wales by the Welsh Books Council www.cllc.org.uk.

Acknowledgements

Thanks to the editors of the following journals and anthologies in which some of these poems appeared in earlier drafts: *Ambit; Dreamcatcher; Envoi; Fire; Magma; nth Position; Orbis; Other Poetry; Poetry Nottingham; Poetry Review; Quattrocento; Staple; Tears In The Fence; The London Magazine; The Reader; The Wolf* and *100 Island Poems Anthology* (Iron Press).

Robin Ford's previous collections are *After The Wound* and *Never Quite Prepared For Light*, published by Arrowhead Press.

Contents

On the Brink

for James & Emma

On the Brink

Asyla

From Pole to Pole

That haunted wing, my mind, resonates
with dialogues and litanies, riots
spill along its corridors, doors slam.
You stalk me, ambush me. I try

to fend you off with pills and booze,
make sleep fill up the space left in my bed
but you, dark one, press through
the cracks and splinters in my dreams.

On garish aching autumn days
I force myself into the sun,
a north-west gale pinpricks my eyes
in lanes leeside high hedges.

I shelter from the squalls off sea
with autumn's final butterflies,
ragged but still brilliant
through rain and storm and frost.

Sunlight on the Ceiling

Light flicks on the ceiling
limpid as a welling spring in morning
amber in the afternoon
cobalt at dusk.

This is light I tried to touch as a child
isolated in my bedroom—
it seemed a smiling thing;
this is light that fixed me
as I drowsed with catatonics on the wards
light that still can raise me
when bony fingers knuckle in my neck
and as I slip the slope of years
it stops me choking on their dust.

Audrey at Whitecroft

*Whitecroft was the former county lunatic asylum on the Isle of Wight, later the
psychiatric hospital until it closed in the 1980's.*

They called me Screamer. I do not think I screamed
but it was better not to question them. Sometimes I felt
a great hand squeeze me in my head, condensing thoughts.
One day I saw a stream of unknown honeysuckle words

written lovely on the sky with messages and fiery signs.
Then I did cry out, with joy, till someone slapped me heavily.
I filled with hurt and doubt until I saw before me suddenly
elves and Jesus too and have done ever since. Such times

are deep and beautiful but painful. When I started bleeding
in the schoolroom, a year before I left, they said I was too young
and when a baby came I did not understand why that was sin
nor why they sent me here. They brought a baby crying

to me, boy or girl, forty, maybe fifty years ago. I lived there
with the others and all the ghosts and goblins of the wards
who also roamed the lovely garden walks. I had no words
to make a sense of this and no-one else could see them clear

so some would hit me till I called on Jesus, His sweet name.
Then things stilled in me and I found courage when men in corridors
jumped me, held me down and did me, time after time
and in the grounds. When fights broke out, in common shame

I went to silent rooms with those like me, who lived in dreams
as sunlight fell on them with God's full blessing; there I'd meet
the baby I saw swaddled once, he or she was like a song to me,
yet I could never find the pitch or key to sing its proper tune.

That babe, grown old, might still walk round this town and please
there be soft beds and loving hearts for him or her who was my own.
My world seemed right for me alone; when I felt sad or down
and violence came my way, I could enter it to blessed peace,

a meadow filled with ox-eye daisies, quaking grass and sorrel
with fairies fine as dragon flies. I quickly learned it was unwise to tell
the doctors of this special place because, in envy (their own hell),
they turned the taps on me, brought out syringes, wet towels,

said I was away with birds and so I was and that is how I wished to
                                                    stay
but even birdsong turned to screams which seemed inside of me; then I
was sent into the cells for days, where peepholes watched me, demon's
                                                    eyes.
I wrestled myself quiet, ate filth they pushed at me through long, bad
                                                    days

of stinking rain, carbolic soap and loneliness. But there were
fine times too when nurses, doctors, patients, played cricket
all as one good team against the villages; we girls, cheering every wicket,
sat to sew and knit the afternoon away. It was there

I worked out many patterns. Despite the quarrels and the rifts
among the brutish, there were human beings, doctors, nurses
who balanced out the hatchet faced and scornful ones of curses
who did to you and sneered despite of our own good gifts.

Some, surely angels sent from God, would talk to us as women,
young girls would sing and dance on rounds or at their cleaning.
There were those, both men and women, on the staff whose nature
was like aunts and uncles, not too many, but you looked for them

and when they went off duty waited for the coming battle.
Then we must endure the human fiends, their everlasting shifts,
and I can say, quite certainly, I saw the Devil lunge in them and hoist
his shadowed flag in flint-eyed ones who treated you like cattle,

waited on your awkwardness so they could pounce and criticise;
some there were so bitter they seemed madder than they said we were,
in need of flattery as we of medicine. Times changed and year on year
new drugs came in, frightening but exciting, bringing changes to our
lives

and some did well on them and either way more of us were sent
to the 'community' as it was called, though we had all that here; some
would came back because they felt the hospital was really home,
they missed the laundry work, the shop where what-was-what and they
content.

Beds began to empty out, unused wards grew dusty, birds got in and
died,
old voices rustled dry as paper. Then a nurse, a good one, best of seven,
taught me embroidery. My world lit up. I saw my brilliant heaven
through her, for God has many means to show Himself to us, the open
eyed.

Suddenly I found my voice.

At first I simply wrote my memories, then I knew that I could show
the world my fairies, witches, elves as they appeared to me, make them
for the pleasure of all who looked on them, both friend and enemy,
how dear God's Heaven was, and thus the world, when you were in the
know.

Silks, wools, cottons, they worked with me as if the linen wed the thread.
I grew well, though old. One day they said, *You have your own home now.*
Shocked I left the ward in fear, bid farewell to every flower,
walked down the drive. Then God said, *Audrey, come.* And I was glad.

Whitecroft Revisited 30 Years On

*Acknowledgements to Oakdene Homes brochure for
'The Pines', Whitecroft Park*

A stunning restoration of late Victorian landmark buildings
The prospect pleases —
sylvan setting, gentle hills, the sheep.
Does the cankered orchard still bear bitter fruit?
et in Whitecroft ego

The old wards named for poets: Shakespeare, Browning, T.S. Eliot.
Gascoyne had his time here.
You have to say the place had aspirations and,
according to its times, did good.

Emptied, gutted, soon to be
                                        a unique collection of homes
I look up at the window of the room I had in 1985 and even in the
show apartments wards can still be traced by those who know
                    stunning (that word again) *apartments with period features*
stunning, that was even then a feature,
ECT and liquid cosh — and worse
a hundred years ago, even in my day the padded cells
                                        there will be a style to suit everyone
that was ever true
                    not just somewhere to live but somewhere to enjoy life
some difference there.

The brochure: glamour woman, her husband-pet, he so cute, in
charge of cooking in the *luxury* kitchen (a girl's dream, her on top
with perfume, gin)

We never felt so relaxed,
the high ceilings and big picture windows make the rooms so light and airy.

I remember cobwebs in the corners up so high that some poor souls feared them as nests where 'those things' crouched, ready to swoop down on them like raptors and even now, with all this countryside around, spiders will call in to live in corners hard to reach. Maybe long forgotten lives will send an embassy of ghosts to utter little moans on midnights when those tall, harsh pines beat in the wind.

Asylum Days

Through days he stares at pines
beyond his window
keens along with their harsh songs
in faulty harmony.
Twigs scathe the blood red bricks.

Those broomstick branches
catch and hold the stars on icy nights
when whispers, footsteps, sudden rushes,
haunt the landings.
Knuckles rap his door:

who is it

he neither deigns nor dares
to breach his barrier but runs his finger
round the elmwood architrave:

who is it

the room teems full of life
that feeds on dust beneath the bed
breeds in wainscoting, bright eyed
but never needing breath:

what if it should go away

The New Life

I am cast from Eden
into alien light,
bloodshot moon
struggles to its zenith,
echoes of old harmonies
beat like sails in backing wind.

I must journey roads
regardless of their destination,
not be seduced by open doors
which might open on to frowsty halls,
rancid chambers, charcoal gardens

nor be tempted onto side paths,
snared by two-faced time
and though words spill easy from my tongue
they are my only ballast.

The Energy

What can be done to ride a storm
that streaks away across the brain?
Rein back its tiger energy?

How to still a mind that pours
unstoppable as water over weir?

Might as well seize shooting stars
bright as fish in darkened oceans,
halt the sudden wind that whines
through whin on heath and hill.

I grip and try to hold onto my place
but sometimes, like a plastic bag,
I blow away, get hooked on twigs,
or on unnecessary finials.

Faustus: a sequence

Friday Night with Faustus

bright dreams after dark deals
he makes a ruckus in a pub
bullets fire and fuse him
he fists his brain in black delight

from his wound he pulls
a string of diamonds
snorts lines of amethysts
before a mirror in the gent's urinal
contrives an angle that will let him view
a passage way into his temples
and crouched like Alice wanders tunnels
past knaves and walruses
through nauseous doors

this is what he bought and bargained for
his pleasure come
as piper he commands the company
to dance punk symphonies
jar harmonies across the spheres
in unsuspected universes
he raps poems out in colours
plays with living toys
sews Rothko wounds
in plush and felt

who would not trade soul
for prizes such as these
what's a soul worth weighed against
such atavistic wilderness

Faustus Flies

He flies the skies twice daily
first falls with shooting stars inside his brain
abandons all and joins the birds
soars again to churning clouds
fuelled by Mephistopheles who is The Man
round here.

F. blows kisses to the Brocken Spectre
snorts the snows of Everest,
dances in the deserts of the Moon.
He, poor fool, trusts M's good gear,
skirts cracked ice,
skates wildly through old night,
whoops and ricochets in canyons,
is Phaeton riding out the flaming firmament
drawn by strange and lovely horses.

When, spent and giddy,
he falls back upon his couch,
Daddy M, who keeps to his side of the bargain
while it lasts, mutters hints of refuelled bliss
until Doc F cries out in agony for ecstasy.

But is it Art?

He takes up art to justify those too two dozen years,
the number twenty four begins to sprout its fangs.
Faustus begs great Mephistopheles, (bound as a seal
upon his arm, IT who so obliges bondsmen),
to send him flickers from the gods, fire, afflatus—anything.

This foul and faithful fiend sends down a sooty dove
as messenger and inspiration to this sely knave, so wode,
credulous, pseudo-student of the certainties,
locked keyless in the dungeons of life's universities
and lo, behold and lackaday, a swarm of muses
pester him, writhe, dance, bombard his mind
with ideas addled as an ancient egg—but fashionable:
targets, projects, courses and degrees. He must make

Choice and this is his: the apple goes to *Poesie*,
he plights his troth, but she is *Lamia*, pythoned
in her wroth, who fills his pen with gall. He who would be
Milton, at the least, gains only insight into H-----,
out-trumps mages, sages and every poet fallen to the *Pit*.

In pride he buffs up *Paradise*, its loss, but at what cost?
It is cadenza leading to a grand collapse and *oh* and *oh*
his demons cry and *fie* at such futility. Their eyes burn
eager for his *Fall*, his plunge to fire. And tumbling fast
he sees, far off, dying stars and unguessed galaxies.

Papa Faustus

Time flies on
he has to recognise his shrinking lease

maybe a way to outwit Mephistopheles
who has him trapped in flights and fixes
would be to try the father thing. At least
it would be entertainment for a year or two.

Juiceless he is, but with resource,
drops slivers of his shrunken soul onto
a Petri dish, garbles words the Master taught—
oh what a stratagem.

Oop-la!
fast fruit springs from his old blasted trunk,
a shudder in Jerusalem,
a little darling, snarling thing is born,
astringent fruit that's not quite from his loins.

The babba teethes with ease on razor wire,
is weaned on gin. To F's great shock
he feels both love and pity judder him
(and this may save him yet),
drops a tear for this sour offspring.
Such a thing has not occurred
since magic took him.

Faustus Has Forgotten His Medication

He left his pills at home, wherever that might be.
Three days on, despite the tyranny of pleasures,
small fires and devils flicker at the edges of his eyes,
prance on painted cloth of flame behind him
and another grey and black of soot and cinders
as if he were a mountebank or strolling player.
Is giddy.
His slipping eye refuses focus, carmine tides flood dark canals,
no straws to grasp, he drowns in unrequested fantasies.
Is this a part of bargain or a monstrous trick? Now, poor chick,
it is as if he sailed high seas aboard an upturned table
a curtain rail and single sheet for mast, across the retching waves.
What hope, what hope for those at peril riding choppy sunsets?
How will this fadge?
Can he fetch up beside the place he once called home?
Too rough the night to make it to his study or his brothel.

Who can guarantee no waves will swamp his craft
and should he reach the shores of domesticity
his home might pullulate with stoats and weasels
invading from the wildest woods.

From the Beautiful and Terrible City

In city canyons djinns and devils stir abandoned streets,
high towers flame in evening light,
refulgent birds soar and circle,
bright aircraft scrape the edge of space.

In an office, roseate in sunset, high above the dimming courts,
a sharp-suit man in silhouette bows head against plate glass.

Old silence weighs him down until he screams.

Faustus: His Death

He asks:
is this

   IT?

his lonely babble
just audible

little light
less regret

he waits conclusion

meanwhile weakens
for arms to hold him
a hand to touch
his chilling fingers
a whisper in his failing ear

something to pluck
beside these
white white sheets

a home to die in
not this shiny empty room

hears blackbird singing

Schumann: *Scenes from Faust*

That great dark legend which absorbs the age
obsesses him, he has to write a music
that will stem the flows of cortisol.

It seems that stinging flies wreathe haloes
round his head, he wracks with shivers.
High notes, especially A, appal him,
metals horrify: horns, trumpets, keys.

It takes nine years until he breaks his pen,
throughout he soars and drowns. Perhaps
he suffers the bi-polar or maybe last phase
of the Tertiary, hollow bones, black wens,
maggots tunnelling his mind.

Once he shouts, *Night falls*, and faints,
hears cries that emanate from heads
that roll about dark hills. He is
a ball the gods toss to and fro.

He hurls himself into the Rhine,
revived, is locked away, Clara forced to view him
through a pane of glass in case, the doctors warn,
he'll scream at sight of her. Eternal Feminine
reduced to Gorgon or Medusa.

Two harsh years until the rusty gate
that jails his mind and body scrapes ajar,
allows a sort of freedom into death.

Wight

Island

You see I come from here,
I will not deny the isle nor expel
it from me. Islands either draw you or repel,
hold you tight or wash you onto greater shores.
Indifference not an option, else why stay?

I am from its hills,
swaddled in a web of deep green lanes,
feel sometimes like a figurehead
scanning sea and sky
my Janus face to land and sea.

Islands give themselves to those who let them.
I could never find a new place now
but then, not ever
and though I feel for other places,
when sea small-washes over me
I am driftwood flung ashore and beached again.

Boundaries here are fixed, horizons limitless.

Back of the Wight

Adapted from the book of this title by Fred Mew

I
Preface *to the 1933 edition*

In the hope these tales
of my beloved Island home
may interest others
I pass them on
with apologies for the rough and ready way
they are set down.
I make no pretence
of putting them in shape,
they are like our Island coast
rough and rugged.

II
A Glorious Morning 1913

I sit by Blackgang Chine
four hundred feet above a sea
that's brilliant blue,
a thin, white line of foam
kissing at red shingle beach
which stretches from
St. Catherine's Point up to
the dreaded ledge at Atherfield,
graveyard of many a fine ship.

Cliffs reach to the Needles,
all different shades, lines of ironstone,
water stained called Redstreaks,
black gault, upper, lower greensand,
white chalk cliffs at Freshwater.

A peregrine calls his mate, brooding eggs below,
a raven calls, *Kraak, Kraak,*
unmoved by mobbing jackdaws,
all of them are hunting, splendid birds—
shame on our so-called sportsmen
who love to shoot them.

The Tunnel Boys

This is what it felt like that weekend
when John and Shuff and I
were near our thirteenth birthdays—
we walked the tunnel where empty trains
had given up the route from downs to sea,
ducked barbed wire, scooted past
the cottage where a crossing keeper once lived,
headed for the tunnel portal, balancing on rusty track,
hopping sleepers, ignorant of all ahead,
unsure of things to come but set on reaching them,
edgy when the curve cut light from either end.

We gabbled scary jokes, made whoops and echoes
to keep our courage, never thought of turning back—
suddenly we saw a pinprick light which seemed
unreachable and might stay so forever, then slow,
slow, neared the shocking sun, emerged into
its stunning fall which felt like an anointing,
looked out on brilliant, endless sea,
understood that every wave was there to crest,
that we would master boats to sail,
skirt rocks and maybe wreck on them,
perhaps to reach some semi-promised lands

Playing Coastguards

When we were boys we played around
the coastguard cottages along the lane
where watchers saved a thousand lives
through years. Our game was rescuers

of all whose ships were split on rocks
in squalls. An out of kilter weather vane
still tinks and scrapes beside those tough
low houses, little windowed against gales

in gardens swamped with sea thrift, poppies,
salty grass, where vegetables once struggled.
Now no trained eyes look out at weather's fits,
the cottages are second homes or weekend lets,

no SOS comes stuttering in. But Overners
who buy them unaware, take note: sea gnaws,
cliffs slip, mansions fall to waves, your bones
and bricks might be at peril from the deeps.

Flotsam

Albatross, Sirenia, Irex, Clarendon
They who fish by night bait rods,
snug down to drink and dream,
claim footsteps rasp the shingle—no-one's there,
they drink and dream.
See-Bee, North Star, Friendship, Bluebell
A two-faced lee coast, which does not let a storm trapped ship
tack back to safety; in summer sweet, by autumn
treacherous with storms that break a vessel's back
on reefs and rocks, craft too weak to keep their keels.
Ruined cliffs flump down to beach, undermined by slipper clay.
Apthorp, Juno, Beaumonde, Helgewall
Waters forceful as the maelstrom take many crews
who drown in coils of kelps and wracks. Headlands ever
on retreat funnel currents, outsmart charts and lights:
Fortuna, Virginia, Atlas, Dizzy Dunlop
Such sacrifices made to save the drowning,
memorials in Chale and Brighstone churchyards,
long dead lifeboat crews now framed on walls of pubs
for those who scrambled down the chines when call went out,
ordinary, heroic men and boys, gone to water
later into earth, killed by pressure slumped too low, too fast:
St. Michael, Juanna, Cormorant, Jeans.

We walk the low tide shore; a cloudy day, storm passed,
sand dull and flat. Lugworm casts like walnuts,
knot and dunlin feeding at the water's curl.
Above sea's usual reach a mesh of blowsy rubbish:
cans, plastic, oil, tar-clogged garments, rope.
There's been a wreck along the coast, cargo flicked
off decks, tossed from holds and split containers.
Round the bay a line of heavy duty rubber gloves
gagged up by sea, orange as funeral garlands on the Ganges,
fingers splayed as if cold hands, at last gasp reach, lay dead in them:
Albatross, Sirenia, Irex, Clarendon.

On Chalk

Formed over ages from the sea
hills of scanty topsoil
tight turf under scud of cloud and sun
this my land, sustainer and reviver:

scabious harebell hawkbit
silverweed knapweed clary
thyme and marjoram

sweet wing butterflies
marble-white chalk-blue copper
brimstone comma painted ladies
Glanville's fritillary, our very own

gaudy dusty moths
cinnabar burnet
humming-bird hawkmoth
sly Mother Shipton

and in an abandoned marlpit
when I brush against
bramble dock coltsfoot
where it's claggy
thistle sprung and anthill tussocked
I turn child again

Surf

sea-boys ride on wave crests
skim lives of serious joy
self absorbed as pods of first year dolphins
mesmerised by tides and breakers
from first breath along the shores
of this salt town where they will spend their span
always on the edge of things
riches gleaned from frugal living
season jobs which pay enough
for ale dope chips and love
girls in thrall to one of them at least
who birth and raise a range of kids in winter lets
or squats when summer fills the town
a merry crew laid back among the fashion
which has started coming here
traders dealers A-list stars restoring mansions
villas cottages whole terraces
which not so long ago housed families

these golden lads just hang on in
professors of the wind and tide
whirled in jumbled families dense as sardine shoals
dads and uncles aged to longshore elders
with straggle beards grey hair piercings and tattoos
moored to cosy living on their sagging sofas
driftwood sea floats hung on walls
talismans of all fish suppers

but ears tuned still to music of the wind and wave
gibbous fevers of the moon and cloud
waiting for the next up-boiling thrash of mackerel

Almost Idyll

August beats empty lanes,
singes fields to ochre
flowers purple, gold.

Insects, lizards,
stoked and fired
by swollen sun,
rushes in baked ditches
spill chocolate florets,
thistles by now with tattered wigs,
bend heads to autumn.

It is so quiet
I wonder if I live—
until a whining plane
scrapes like a fingernail
on sapphire glass,
leaving scratchmarks on the sky.

The Panic

On hogback of the hill
contorted hawthorns,
bent crooked by prevailing winds
lie almost level with the earth
suppleness turned knots and gnarls.
They endure gales, sough in faintest breezes,
even on a calm day
there is a susurration in the branches
when a freshet passes.

Up here it seems earth lies open
to its heart; you might encounter Panic,
that great god who does not live
in unknown places but in elements
unknowable. For a few seconds
dark joy overwhelms.

Alone in the House

With you away the house is silent
as a midnight monastery

moon spreads lemon light across my bed
gale has passed but waves still break
with flagging force
gnaw this landfall of the endless ocean

my inmost seas ebb out
then flow to flood me
till I rise
drawn by a silver string
up to the ghostly warmth storms trail

I hover over ships and houses
where hearts beat slow
as embers in banked fires

foxes run to different pulses in the woods
all is fragile but the sea
whose waves uncoil
with force of ferns

to these simple energies
I slip to sleep

At Dimbola in Freshwater

home of Julia Margaret Cameron, pioneer of photography

Mrs Cameron: her hobby turns to passion,
she summons up her pride of lions, cajoles, teases them
till they comply with visions of her inner eye,
she white hot, fired at her homely forge of inspiration.
A blacked out henhouse round the back is darkroom,
Her hands stained dark with chemicals.

Tennyson of course, a private path and gate for him
from Farringford, all the fashionable and great
who take up Freshwater: Browning, Darwin, Millais,
happy to pose as kings and mythic figures, Dodson's
Alice, staying up the road, whole lot fixed for us
by silver nitrate. Wondering fisher kids, all snot
and scales, transformed to angels, fitted out
with wings ripped off dead geese and martyred swans.
Ellen Terry on the brink of everything, beautiful as dawn.

What jinks. The great and good at play, Watts at paint,
a passing visit by the Queen in dogcart. But also
swarms of wasp-like tourists, early groupies, gather
to gawp at talent and celebrity, poking heads
through hedges, spying on the teas and picnics.

The great ones will accept the end of Wonderland,
too much stirring of their nests. Sudden flight
to work and play in quieter corners of a shrinking world.

In Clerken Lane

Hollowed by centuries of trudge from priory to castle,
further carved by rain through thickets
of beech uncoppiced hazel, ash,
epochs of fallen leaves mulched down to richness,
a maze of paths on either side, trod by kids, their dogs,
my own feet years ago.

Fooled by nostalgia I leave the main way, totter
on a muddy tightrope of a track, ridged high, slippery
with autumn, find it now cut short mid-way, mid-air.
I hesitate, shuffle down as best I can
slip-tumble-aaargh—soft landing, not hurt at all
but like a beetle on its back I look through trees to sky,
my world awry, nothing fits and upside down I realise

this was a silly search for some lost perfect time,
an ideal only years and memories allow
and yet, lying longer than I need to, I feel one with littered leaf
beneath me and mutter to myself that this might be
a place to lie forever, children's feet above me in their play.

But moods don't last,
the beech trees seem to whisper
in voices of the enigmatic ones and warn:
who says can't know, who knows can't say.

On the Brink

The Leather Women of Lytes Cary

Lytes Cary House is near Frome in Somerset

We are, you might say, greeters,
our place is in the entrance chamber of the house.
We have leather lips, leather tongues, leather eyes.

No-one knows who made us
or why they did, or when—
no more do we.

Though leather-clad in Restoration style,
the guidebook has us sewn and tooled
a century later on. Why does it say this?

Forever here, yet we feel lost.
Were we made to scare off thieves
(oh we'd make 'em run)
or, in case thirteen sat down at table
so we could make up numbers,
keep whatever beast they feared away?
Our presence might deflect the dread
of night time knocks
or rushing wings in chambers.

We are cousins to the dummy boards,
silent companions, distant relatives
of puppets, manikins, automatons;
old, stiff-lipped. We keep our place
but have no way to voice our thoughts.
Inwardly we speak the local accent.

One day a visitor might come
to free us from our silence.

        Is it you?

Do You Know the House?

Look at that house.
Perhaps it is your house.
What do you see?

A woman motionless behind her pane
a man one floor below beating at his window,
arms drag him back.

Wind sucks curtains out
of open windows, they flap
like ostriches attempting flight,

doors and rooms inside
might well be sealed
corridors impassable,
stuffed with screwed up papers,

there may be suites of gilded chambers
each with an imprisoned beauty,
out of reach.

Look at this house.
Did you live there once?
Does part of you remain within it?

Pleasaunce

You have reached this garden
it is mine but you were not to know

in this place men and women
live in fantasies and legends
but children have no need of it

you seem happy to be here
but look on carefully
see another garden
and glints of more along
a tunnel lane

let birdsong guide you
past fearful thresholds
under arches
in search of ever greater beauty.

You will not find your perfect garden
the one you dream about
there is no final garden
even so
better that you search for it

hear breeze
imagine lyres.

Words to One Who Went Away

Why did you choose that gateway
in the wall when you ran off?
Did you find the soaring life
or wander all the high roads
of the world? I no longer see
your face but can't forget
your tarry hair was beautiful.
Do you recall the passers-by
your eyes once hooked before
you threw them, gasping fishes, back?

Apologies and doubts hatch out
like midges in my mind; I live
my little world but long to tell you
how things go and, though our times
are like dried blood, I relive them
in my waking times. My voice fails.
From your distance you are silent.

I am bound for highways for a season,
I doubt we'll meet but should fate
snare a trick don't turn, I beg you,
leave me to linger in strange shadows
as I watch sunsets over motorways
gold and purple with pollution.
Do you, like me, live evenings
dreaming of next morning's light?

Snake

he could trigger earthquakes
in the vulnerable
like me

jewelled snake
leather   shades   tan
though not my usual type
his Donatello pose provokes

he looks like rent
for either sex or any taste
gigolo
louche and dangerous
as a Cardinal's catamite
jutted hip   tight ass
forked glance

snorts a line   smokes a rock   shoots up
me the timid fantasist of gutters

but no Orton I
me country boy
small town boy
outsider boy
no longer boy at all

pass by
he dangerous
me scared

An Uncomfortable Truth

An article in the journal Nature *(January 2007) describes incidence
and frequency of homosexual behaviour in the animal kingdom*

A truth uncomfortable to some is this:
fifty species at the least of bird and beast
will swing both ways; thirty seven, more or less,
in every hundred seahorses go gay,
whales do it man to man, it is their way,
on rolling waves in view of ocean cruises
(nervous passenger avert their gazes).
Giraffes go at it next to roads (a photo shows)
and feel no shame, mussels cluster on each other
in their scores, each bi-sexual, shoot their sperm
and eggs out millions at a time, no bother,
to sweep across the reaches of indifferent seas.

It could be all these common acts are consequence
of little genes which went in such and such a way
right from the wormy start of things. *Tendency*
as it is sometimes claimed, might come from nurture,
though I would say seahorses grow in random play
to live out lives of gay abandon, according to their nature.
Who knows why Walibri men, deep in the heart of Oz,
on meeting shake each other's penises—but so it is.

Oscar in Old Street

I catch his scent by Smithfield where air
once stank with dead beast's blood —
imagine stalactites of tallow, dynasties of flies.
Butcher's lads who worked the meat racks
liked a gent who paid and threw in dinner.
Thrill, endurance, foolishness and pride
cast sainthood of a sort on him.

His phantom touches me. I feel his pulse
in neighbourhoods around St. Luke's,
walk by him on this hot and horrid Sunday.
Baking walls absorb and hold the air,
his spirit spooks the niggled lanes off Old Street,
passes yards which reek of rot, of mouse and oil,
where gutters leak in storms and walls weep moss.

Day melts slow as sealing wax but we two,
he and I, are suddenly alert to hot, hard,
driven souls who whisper *follow me.*
His spirit quickens and my body with it.
    We both obey.

A Distant City

Honey pot, you set up traps
for lads and lambs
of every inclination.

The moon drowns stars
as I walk beside the sticky river
little demons at my shoulder,
I seek gardens and a cooling breeze
and oh, I lie.

Up unlit lanes, high walls hide courtyards,
men with smiles invite you past the gates
to smoke-and-mirror-rooms of concrete floors
and dirty mattresses
where little goddesses with pointy eyes
whoop ululations in praise of Innocence
the bland
whose other name is 'He betrays'.

And later
flight past ruined walls
over wastes lit sharp as scimitars
by old man moon,
mind ploughed and harrowed
as the irrigated fields,
back to the town I once supposed
was near to Eden or to ancient Ur.

Mycenae

The music of the palace
      unanchored by notation, is lost
           in hillside winds above the plains of Argolis.

Clay tablets now deciphered
      yield only household details in lost tongues
           they may be read but never heard.

What do they mean
      the elemental smiles of votive images?
           I cannot read their huge dark eyes.

Crowds swarm the sacred places
      I walk away along a track
           to shadow, breeze and silence.

Beneath a shrubby oak a turquoise lizard
      darts through poppies,
           golden sedge and grass

I feel at one with all the world
      afloat in word and thought
           beyond all music

Dead Gods

In the long gallery
gods with piss-hole eyes in ruined faces
meet my gaze.
Faint horns, flutes, lyres,
skitter in the chambers of my ears,
with echoes of blood-greediness. They
are kin to those blank-eyed and beautiful,
whose smiles are terrible, also to the ones
who hide in clouds.

Those that wrought them
are now dust in winds but their works,
though damaged, stay pregnant,
primed for crazes, cults, enthusiasms
latent in the fearful.

I know their powers and charms,
they crouch at my mind's margins
and though this lot will soon go down
into the oubliettes and vaults
they can wait for times to turn
their way again.

Hares

Crouched in set-aside and stubble
they birth leverets in scrapes called 'forms'
streak across the tilth of open fields,
disappear like witches, sprites, shape-shifters
gifted with invisibility,
their coats and coverts trick the eye.

Reputed to be lovers of the moon,
servants of Eostre, protected by Saint Melangell,
they tease our submerged fantasies.
We read them carelessly, suppose
hares box for sport or territory in spring
whereas such skirmishes are females
fending off the over-eager males
before the oestrus is complete.

I like to be a maggot to a myth,
gnaw to know the what, the how, perhaps the why?
but that's in day; on any night I'll slip bounds
when gales beat trees and wild sea crashes shore,
black dogs bark
and demons lope and curl on vaulting horses
round the lumber rooms inside my mind where life's detritus,
stashed away since childhood, moulders,
never tidied up or thrown away,
a place where hares stay magical
till I fall back to what might be, in part,
my proper, duller, mind.

The Latest Restoration

My final portrait?   I doubt it
just the latest overpainting.
It does for now.
I like it.

The original? A daub,
canvas ill-prepared, brush strokes
coarse—there's little left
of that attempt.
Paint from every restoration
shows the taste
of diverse generations.

But do you mark faint outlines—
myself as youth? My eyes seem fixed
on distant slaughter in an ideal garden.
Experts will note
charcoal marks that hint a skull
staring out behind my shoulder,
mocking my filled and furrowed face.

I Knew Bartok

You don't believe me, jibe I am too young?
Our lives overlapped by three full years,
my first, his last, even though I never was
in Hungary, nor exile in the USA (war and youth
is my defence). But I heard the muted sounds
of wilderness, creaks, cries in midnight woods,
with him whose hearing was phenomenal—
bat calls, owl shrieks, grubs burrowing in logs.

Once I dreamt the two of us set sail in boats
gunnel-full of those on vague but potent pilgrimage
to seek the seals. He longed to hear the songs ascribed
to selkies, blocked off by limits of the usual human ear.
Despite the whirr and click of cameras and though
the seals were silent, I think he sensed their song
and I was feared, as it is sometimes said, they might
assume a human form, lure him to the sandbanks
of the Wash or far-flung skerries in the wild north-west.
But he was more of land than sea and maybe sounds
that hug the ocean's heave are waves on frequencies
other than the ones he heard, and sing in different tunes.

I knew him, know him still, despite his death in exile,
there is no bar to knowing artists such as he. That harsh
music flows to me from him, preserver of the melodies
and harmonies his century killed, peasant songs and dances,
Magyar, Bulgar, Roma, rescued from the deaths
and silence of the camps so I, and you if you should
take to them, may sing them still. When I walk lanes
at dusk, gaze at stars above both woods and sea,
I feel him strong as running waters. Should you
doubt our friendship I say *hear me* and stutter out
a phrase so feebly, you turn away. His rhythms,
irrepressible as springs, are plasma to me, inexhaustible
despite the great felled forests and the windy plains
which birthed and sheltered them till Europe fell and died.

Valhallas

In Brezhnev's time I travelled to Lake Ritza
in the Caucasus. As I went up the sheep and goats
were coming down for winter in the lowlands,
their bells rang through the valley sweet as carillons.

A mile beneath Mount Elbruz' peaks I saw
the lake: turquoise water, recent snow, vast
forests. What drew the eye was Stalin's
favourite mansion in this, his native land.
Fourteen years since he had died in his own piss.

I have seen home movies shot by Eva Braun
at Hitler's Wolf's Lair, parties so *gemutlich* that,
for the moment, I saw the glamour in power divorced
from consequence, high above plains of bloody soil
and orchards rich in bones of murdered Jews.

From the Ashes

Ten years after truce. Houses
still wrecked or poxed by war.
Fireweed thrives in scathed soil
rich in ashes, graves and soot.

Women set up roadside stalls again,
sell honey, cheese, plum brandy
hot as new fired guns or age old feuds,
to coaches pausing fifteen minutes
for tourists to purchase souvenirs.

Soon they leave the plains to climb
karst valleys sharp as sudden death,
up to blissful lakes where maybe
no gun fired nor blood was shed,
or if it was, all's one now
and humus by the pure streams.

The Oxus, the Indus and the Aral Sea

When I am well again I will lie on a chalk hillside,
breathe calmly, turn my head to see sunset fall

on sedge, burnet, harebells, float on scent of thyme
and marjoram; spring will warm my bones and over me

crossbow swifts will wheel and tumble. My eyes
will rejoice with hawkbit, speedwell, scabious,

bloodspot orchids will be the only stain the world knows,
my mind will be a new hatched butterfly

testing unexpected wings. When I am strong I will fly
to the Indus and Oxus, I will fill again the Aral Sea

to proper bounds, cleanse it, fill it with fish again
for I sense miracles in these oscillations, like those

strange landscapes I wandered in my storm of sickness.
And if I can resurrect the Aral Sea, why not try

to conjure into form those I loved, even the dead
and disappeared, so that they pass in frieze along

the lovely, ancient lane? When I call they will turn
and smile on me and their eyes will smile also.

At First Light

Trees have hinterlands no freshet can disturb

in rocks and fissures next to springs
lizards wait for warmth

one grey minute
takes an hour then radiance of tangerine
suggests the sun

when it heaves itself above horizon
it silvers samphire on the cliff
gilds summer grass

birds declaim their territories
gulls on shore stir in their scrapes
launch off to scavenge
cormorants flex to dive

I might be first human on the scene
brain primed to shift preceding balance,
of innocent but complex mind
hard-wired to tip the world from kilter.

A Walk on Iona

the true mystery of the world is in the visible, not the invisible
— *Oscar Wilde*

a thin place
which some suggest lies on God's frontier
all I can say to this is
      being is my meaning
I can be at one with things
when light falls   *thus*

rare soft sunlight
many seafowl
eight rams in a dry stone paddock
fatten for the tup

The 'Road of the Dead'
leads from Abbey to the graveyard
a one-way street *ho-ho*
here the nudge of death is not so terrible

we sail for Staffa
dolphins cleave swell beneath our sober little boat
leap and scud
merry as the lucent day
glint and dazzle in glassy sea,
the vessel bucks
as we move side to side
      asking for their—

oh today the sea is a gem
we seem to swoop with seabirds

On the Road from Cordoba to Granada

The year is out of touch with rain
wells dry,
stubble crackles on scorched hills
smoke pennons
flicker over ochre towns

fire engulfs an orange grove
sap boils and whines
things cannot stand or stay,
white fish bones
thread and trace lost river beds
but stubborn thorns resist,
sink deep roots
draw up hidden waters.

Let me be as they are
not in imitation only
but touching life deep down

I will sing songs of living
pour libations down to aquifers,
revive the life that I let slip.

Thunder in the Garden

You say birds sing in worlds
beyond your reach,
our lives run parallel.

If we made love
would that connect us ?
(I scheme where pleasure
is concerned)
Not now, you say.

Thunder clouds
blunder up from France,
thick as fog banks over sea,
they cannot hold their rain.

It is a stormy summer,
grass grows sick with wet,
a fever season shot with bolts,
flowers furred with cankers.

Together Clinging

'We two lads together clinging'
—*Walt Whitman*

for James

We've seen it, haven't we? I mean,
not all, but quite enough. Survived
the wrecks, clung to bowsprits,
washed up on rocks.
We've helmed it past the sirens
till now, with time and age, we find
our berth in loving-kindness, know
for us it is the better way to live.

But things move on,
death rattles like a distant army on the move,
must one day separate our hearts
that took so long to join,
and afterwards the other has to walk
the shifting sands of frailty and failing mind.
How foolish not to have a family, but then
no Regan and no Goneril—
no facile talk dispels the fears.

September at Clun

The swallows sense the pull of Africa,
some will not survive the flight
from hemisphere to hemisphere—
gunfire, deserts, lie ahead—
yet most will come to Clun again.

They dive and soar around the castle ruins,
too swift for me to follow any bird,
swoop, electrons round a nucleus,
aligned in one great swing of energy.

Seeing them as light begins to fail,
my restless mind gains calm; suppose
each swallow took a thread, carried it
through loops and spins to weave a cloth
that knit our fractured world to harmony.
But as dark falls I think about Penelope,
the web she wove through day, and which,
each night, she had to rend apart.

And Did You Get What You Wanted From This Life, Even So?

Raymond Carver

It was you might say
a patchwork quilt
of gathered scraps
tacked randomly
clashing colours snatched from skips
from dreams and daylight robberies.

The stitching was my own
imperfect, primitive,
I was always awkward at such things
but persevere—
to what end you must judge

My hands were clumsy, tangled,
I was bad at threading needles,
could not tell the hooks from eyes.

Now holes appear, stitches snap,
moths move in—
yet it hangs together somehow,
keeps me warm.

In answer to your question

    I did   I do

On the Brink

You, who night sweats swiftly drowned,
brought me to these fragile shores
spiked and speared by marram grass
whose wiry roots hold back the waves.

The landscape took my breath away—
church towers stark as ships at sea,
dykes, fields, marsh. When you spoke
I, impatient, answered sharply back.

These lands are tough, life balances
on cusp of wind and tide. In lee of dunes
oak and ash bow heavy crowns, stunted
by salt wind harsh as hail, or by driven sand.

Landside in summer, barley all but malts
on stem, roadsides are gaudy with poppy,
mallow, tansy, they crowd and jostle for the sun,
ancient, common plants, forever fresh.

I come back when I can, grieve your final season,
that deadly virus, thick as pollen, clogging up
your lungs, skin lesions all the flowers you bore,
you battered as the beaten coast, breaching
even as I turned and looked the other way.